SOJURNERS

SOJOURNERS

POEMS BY

ANDREW JARVIS

WAYFARER BOOKS
BERKSHIRE MOUNTAINS, MASS.

WAYFARER BOOKS

WWW.WAYFARERBOOKS.ORG

© 2022 TEXT BY ANDREW JARVIS

Cover Design and Interior Design by Leslie M. Browning
Cover Image: © David Billings
First Edition Trade Paperback 9781956368093

10 9 8 7 6 5 4 3 2 1

The Strait
Landslide
Blood Moon

For Betty

CONTENTS

Origins

Ashes

Renascence

ORIGINS

THE ACCEPTANCE

We fled when fields caught fire
and wheat burned to soot,
so father scraped sky
and bled out its buildings
for us, for a city.

Carpenters were for hire,
and father knew of nails:
box, common, masonry,
brad, roof, duplex, drywall,
he nailed knowledge skills.

All for minimum wage,
working without bonus,
he would burn skin in sun
and weld for us, working
to welcome our new home.

Bare, he made us belong
with subway tickets, shoes
with comfort soles, to walk,
congested, where trains sank
farmers in city fold.

XO TASTE

Cantonese, with some creatures
not discussed until college
and a bottle of tequila,
broken open and fermenting

into jellyfish and cuddles,
objects resembling tongues,
and squiggles of pig intestine,
the special is tomorrow.

But today is yesterday's love,
effervescent, fogging the air,
like nuclear power at sea,
radiating fish and frying

a route to a reception desk
with smitten men, so welcoming.
They pinch the air like lobster claws,
waving, and pointing out their tank.

Of unidentifiable
amorphousness, they white red
and splattered brown, acidic,
like burning skins in sun, split

and releasing an aroma
so rank that even a server
falls into its froth, to spotlight
a brave face of gold, but brighter.

ANTIQUE RAT

White Staffordshire spaniels
wear laces of black and red
roses within Sterling
silver settings of fork
and knife rosaries, splayed
so prongs point to ceiling
Baccarat chandeliers
that enlighten cases
of collectible china,
Lenox and Spode saucers,
servers, platters, pitchers,
each with pastel flowers,
hand-painted, blossoming,
beside candelabras,
embroidered napkins,
emerging over bowls
in a polished stage
to reflect a porcelain
Limoges vase on view,
with pink, yellow, and white
roses, permanently
stemming from the center
of royal arrangement,
representing a proud
permanence in this shop
of regal valuables—
when rodent crawls from it,

paws its pastel petals,
slips on sepals, and breaks
through glass, catapulting
off cutlery to dogs
who cannot bark it off
delicate coats, crashing
on the oriental
rug, discounted for you,
while storeowners howl.

HOUSE DRINK

He bottled it up, with glasses
and chalices for beer and wine,
a house of drunken pleasure.

He collected conversations
of wives, marriages, and affairs,
speeches, bottled, enwombed.

Manipulative mothers, sons
who violated evening
curfews, they all drank like gutters.

Fathers, daughters, distant lovers
and their beneficial friends,
they pour into his glass dwelling.

Home, he wanted this sight, to gulp
confessions, see humans caught
in drunk sentiment, recycled.

CASTLE BREACH

Father taught me walls of concrete
to build our mouse king a castle

with baited dungeon, killing trap,
to rid his house of my vermin.

He hunted my childish demons
with breath of carnivorous heat

to eat up their misbehaviors,
bound in my breeder, untamed.

Tormented with mallet, I hit
his prison to pebbles, grounded,

so I could make creatures like me,
dreamer of wombats and weevils

in kingdoms of enchanted beasts,
born, from his building, dethroned.

GRILLING MONUMENT

The grill is smoking rain
after summer, in fall,
when our grandfather thought
water would wash away
his waste, his afterburn
of burgers, hotdogs, buns,
charred to morbid black,
as if dynamite blew
meat to sculptures, ashen
piles, fuming waves of wind
that chimed into mold,
hanging high above, caught
when he passed, yet he
refused to remove
that tumor, monument
of mistakes, temperature
trove of family disgust,
his well done, never raw.

HOW GROWNUPS FIRE

Father taught us to shoot
in swamps, where still water
forced us to balance
in bogs, keeping the stocks
snuggled in shoulder bones,
between bodies and chins,
to extend our third arms
and gauge the ways of geese,
to aim ahead and eye
their wings, while we waded,
waiting for flight, rigid
snipers with barreled shots,
ready for bird bolting,
before wind awakened
squall, shot water to sky
and sank us, saving birds
in bluster, sinking guns
into gushy mud, mire
where father grappled us
with his threatening grip
and threw us wimps ashore,
disowning his children
as cowards, always weak,
while he slipped on slugs, shot
his feet, and fell, watching
us master the misfire.

FAMILY RACER

Alternators, carbonators,
bearings, blocks, blowers, and filters,
list for his little engine things
for grandfather to pay for, not

college or a new computer,
but rather radiators, rods,
starters, and water pumps, play toys
for grandson's glory, family speed,

supercharged, he throttles up
for his driver of dreams, to be
superspeedway champion, eating
surf and turf with trophies for forks

and medals for plating, player
of women in the owner's box
above his track, where grandfather
gave the world to him, hopelessly

showering spoiled rotten things
for absent advanced degree,
but rather bras, thongs, high-heeled
women draping over his drag

for an automotive god, girls
gawking below, for a picture
of the family line, limitless
spenders on sensational toys

of ineptitude, breaking down
in grease, where relatives gear up
for gold medals, then melt away
in synthetic tires, crashed, gone.

STUFFING MAN

Attic bow, it is father's cross,
curving around his son's body:
a boy in a cathedral of heads.

Wild boars, eagles, mountain elks,
they watch the room, bewildered
by its blooding, the heart of it.

He climbs between the string and arc,
as if an arrow to heaven,
to shoot himself into angels.

In wild, where his daddy went
to pummel the beasts by poaching
his wildlife prizes, priceless.

He plunders them, rips heads off walls
and wears them as masks, to mimic
animal sight, before shooting.

Father enters, worshiping son,
his mature taxidermist, man
artistic and proud, preserved.

HERCULES

Bicycle, he believes its bend
is a symbol of suffering.

Bones, bruises, hernia surgeries,
he recollects them like trophies.

Golden, with Grecian engravings
of muscled gods, he's Herculean.

Sun shadows behind him, bending,
when skateboarder smashes mighty.

Highwayman from Hades, he hits
the hero out of him, gallantly.

With pimpled gamer grin, torn jeans,
and smoke-it-up shirt, it's all good.

And Hercules is paved, prostrate,
because that's awesome shredding, man.

VULTURE HOUSE

Buzzard besieged birds
in lofted house, empty,
stole its sparrows away
into burrows of mice,
muzzled, with nightcrawlers
squirming on broken wings
that once flew airs up there.

Filthy, father barked it,
chopped it down, fed it
to his old wood chipper
for fresh flower beds,
because he cannot stand
bird frolic in airflow,
their fondling of breezes.

Vulture, he became one
today, a preying bird
in golden sun, stolen
for his home improvements,
like those detritus birds
that feast on dead couture.

Swiftly smashed, he left
only fodder of home,
hashed nests of nestlings
and bits of birds of prey,
the ones that he praises
for pecking wings apart,
because chips are better.

BEE STING BODY

Head, thorax, abdomen,
antennae with compound
eyes, with a spiracle

behind the wings and jaw,
in our watermelon
today, tempting bee black

and yellow colors, bright
on red with fresh water,
it wants it more than us.

Ocelli and a tongue,
licking impeccable fruit,
beloved, like a heart

in an athletic chest,
pumping out pulp today,
it avoids our orange

cheddar and green pickles
for that sugary sweet,
ripe, unavoidable.

In our pollinated
picnic, with lemonade
and salad, father flips

burgers, benevolent,
vested, like a hungry
vulture, hissing beer,

enabling the aroused
insect, his injected
ouch, scientific.

SLINGSHOT BOYS

Yard of no yielded
hurls, unstoppable hands,
it carries crowded shards
of nevermore nests, gone.

Robin eggs ended here,
drops of opulent blue,
as if formed by sky
fall, splattered, flooded.

Boys blasted them, slingshots
aimed for acute offs
of all sizes, to see
the airspeed of offspring.

Chicks, forced into flight,
downed, for delicate
trophies, they are grounded,
for young aspiration.

To be first, the winners,
champions of birding,
hunters with eggshell crowns,
nested, in fowl needles.

WICKED POOL

Mom detested swimming
so we dug her a pool
with a deep end, to dive
for her, to her chagrin.

Cannonball, bellyflop,
unfathomable flip,
we synchronized mistakes
to become her stubborn.

And she shouted at us
and our unruly acts
of unsafe, uncertain
death, our wet defiance.

Louder with every leap,
she made untamable
monsters, boisterous, bound
to wreak mother's havoc.

We loved her for this:
time of her attention
on the untamed, wild,
as we were the wicked.

WORK TRUCK, TETHERED

Ivy weaves through its wheels
without father nearby
to weed it away, all
shades of green, growing up
from our garden of grease,
oil, antifreeze, and tar,
a raceway in our yard
for the finish of it,
a family pickup truck
with blue and pink ribbon
and a thick rubber spare
mounted over the bed,
where we rode, unbuckled,
in loads of paint, shovels,
cement, hammers, trowels
to our daily jobsite
where we bridged islands
with steel arches and arms,
built by our construction
firm which he formed
for a living for us,
to ride in that rooted
Ford to concrete our work,
never driving away.

PIER GHOSTS

It is frigid in matting fog,
where a fisherman in sardines

pulls his nightly plunder to pier
in a mechanical motion

of buckets, interwoven hands
and handles, clocking sunrise hours.

Onyx and umber, they resemble
ceremonial urns, shimmered

by water in reflecting light,
hoisted by weary arms, a wake

for empty sea, overfished
by his netted grip, grappled.

And moving in tow, as if guts
became bucketed ghosts, squished

together into haunted punch,
flavored by salty, putrid skins,

caught, in his perpetual carry
of souls after sea death, for life.

EXCURSIONS

This morning fishermen hook salmon,
sablefish, smelt, and crab, with otters
teething clamshells, seagulls flying over,
while geese observe the daily work
of market florists, cooks, beekeepers,
handymen, booksellers, and tarot
card readers, all working for minimum
wages, eating bakery flops, and pitching
sales speak, all orders for living.

Across from cruise deals, discounts,
and flash sale fares for every type of cabin
to feel Alaskan inlet air, while watching
glaciers crack under bears feeding
on Copper River spawn, berries,
and caribou that worship Aurora
Borealis, magic in immersive
nature, while being a local
in the eternal sun.

ASHES

OSTEOLOGY

Cranium, mandible, and ribs,
pelvis scattered in femurs,

this is no owl, but obstacle
abstract for the foraging bear

that sheared off feathers, then tore
the meat, the muscles of flying.

For it, the delicious red,
welling over the tongue, to lap

airborne essence, overbearing
in animal fountain, to fill

hibernation, its cloying night,
through this naughtiness.

And here they lie, casual bones,
nonsensical lattice, for lips,

teeth, a jarring jaw, an easy
meal for great mammal, eaten

and broken away, leaving
his pile, our particulars.

HIGH RISE LORE

We set out Sasquatch food: frozen
strawberries, breaded fish sticks, cod,
the best for our city creature.

It will mount our high, rise in quake,
and stomp with bulbous feet, squashing
sidewalk people, their leaden way.

Beast will howl like a twisted horn
of bone and skulls of beaver kill,
barbaric, fracking our top floor.

Eat us, foam teeth, stench air, feast flesh,
so we can dissect your bowels,
the build of bigfoot, folkloric.

In intestines, thorax, stomach,
digest ordered apartment,
make us udder, wilderness gut.

SERENITY LAKE

Ibis in sun equity
it mines for a marine
worm in morning, before
night crawls after moonrise.

Swamp becomes aggregate
sea of stone manure,
risen into a rife
of avian, chaotic.

Stuck in stiff, a gaggle
of them are guzzled, caught
in toad and snake entrails,
slabbed, by nature's caulk.

Then a bull, a dozer
with beastly incisors
rampages white, wrecking
feathers, for purity's float.

Wiped out, no water
walkers remain, only
pools, siphoned of foul fowl,
for serenity swans.

RAINBOW SPLIT

Oil, its rainbow swallows up
sidewalk outside ice cream parlor

in streaks of translucent green
and blue swizzle, like carnival

grease after dyeing candy corn,
brighter than the sherbet inside

the glimmering case of orange,
lime, and raspberry icicles.

And you may find yourself within
its slicker-than-snow-cone blossom,

its orb spiraling into you,
as you slip in overdriven,

its polish for car people
who crave its metallic color

waves, waving like the banana
split behind, in yellow and red

glimmer; you are sucked into slime,
driven, by that lickety-split.

COMMUTING

Up until now
tire marks treaded
on interstates
in empty lanes
within rural
quiet country
of calming corn
in freedom's speed
without sirens
blaring behind
or patrolling
police and guns
chasing robbers
of stolen cars
and illegal
deals of drugs
in city smoke
over tire prints
outside our door
in a wallop
of traffic wrecks
while we wonder
why we don't drive
away and leave
these lanes for them
and their fighting
before father
declares it's time
to drive to school
in warring streets
without limits.

PAINFUL REMINDER

The dentist says implants
are screwed into bone,
and some glue to the gums
to comfort shallow jaws,
offering all sizes
and heights, including widths,
like the nonuniform
fish across the room, rank
of fluoride and feed
that sank into their tank
and canvassed a plaque
of green and brown ugly,
a mesh of aquatic
mold and quagmire
goo that amasses thick
mucous and crude
cakes of curvaceous
sewage, the serpentine
sludge of an ignored
pool of angels, before
he beckons you to him
to drill in all your bits
so you can bite again
and swallow the swimming
of wretched creatures
that pulse in a putrid
waiting room, while you
are in pain and peeking
at those forgotten fins,
which you would never eat
with immaculate teeth,
and your dentist knows that.

SPOILED CRAB

Where turtles swallow straws
and forks pitch in flounder,
an anchored cook breaks
carapace punctures.

He is a king of knives
and plastic pulsations
of cutlery, crabbing
shanty nearby, awake.

He guts a decapod,
its intestinal green,
to scoop out a spoon, bent
and bursting ovaries.

Glands, gills, muscles, midgut,
he slices it, splitting
crustacean in two,
to platter its killer.

Its polypropylene
crust, mantle, gutted core,
he prepares it, serving
crab crackers, fresh spoils.

UNDERGROUND INCOME

Look at the hills, hundreds of mounds,
as if rising to mountains,

moles root our lawn to volcanoes
with craters becoming burrows.

Unbelievable nuisance,
we bought a rifle, a long one

to bullet the beasts, to scare them
away, walling their bloody wells.

But our neighbor, he uses noise
to defend his drooling, his want

of their warming hides, possible
petticoats, and furry cloakings.

He bats them, placing his body
between us and his genuine

garments, his nature for sale
in furs, purses, and hats, his haul.

It is free for us, so we grow
them, let the buggers be, our gift

to the world, for their wonderful
warmth, wealth, and our clearing.

TURTLE, UNSHELLED

He embodies the box,
a boy in a garden alive
with pure allegories

of innocence at fault,
the reptilian fling
of juvenile jest,

gallant and sinful;
he is shucking turtle,
breaking the spine of it

into cavernous blood,
coalescing on grass
and spearing blades in gore,

his opulent gifting,
abandoning his boy
to grow from bloody raw,

maturing in gutted
nightfall. He is gifted,
deshelling shelled life.

BODY OF MINE

Quagmire, he sees monsters
in Mesozoic mass, matted
creatures in gassy greenhouse
dinosaur and foliage fumes,

Neanderthals from ape
evolution, muted by millennia fold,
released in his rocky eruption.
Coal, a creature of geological age,

ashes of mountain quakes,
ends of conifer and deciduous
roots, wound in blasted wall;
he lives by it. Touching

points, he picks
over wealth, thicker
than paper; there is
no money here, only mass

of earthen history; he grips
its blasted black, opened
after green banked gainful
employment, a family of four,

and a Ford. He is fortified
in here, so flees to leave
ages alive in elemental mine,
while earth is layering.

BEACH BURIAL

Clams, cod, rockfish, sanddabs, and sole
bake within smorgasbord dawn.

They offer themselves to the deer
picking over night's aftermath.

Blue and brown camouflage, netted
by green, fish lost to animal.

Biting geoducks and sea gore,
torn by raging tide, it has won.

Then a wave breaks it, shattering
bottles on shore, thrown into skin.

Beer to blood. glass to gut, it falls
onto beach, rocks piercing like spikes.

Sudden surrender, it has lost
ocean war, unforgiving wet.

At sunrise, with shadows casting
scars on slain brawn, water buries.

OILED REFRAIN

Inside the inside of water,
whales create a pitch of red
salmon, otters, orchestrated
in this passage of permanence.

Beluga, walrus, lions, seals,
unrestrainable, surrounding
our cedar canoe, with seaweed
crust, oil slick, they are calling.

Muted, without a maelstrom
for echolocation seeing,
they are not howling harmony
of Alaskan way, deafening.

Royals on rainbow slick, they reign
blue, green, silver, and gold volumes
atop no torment or torture,
as is blissful, a silent sound.

CROW'S NEST

Crows have conquered the lighthouse,
coated its light with dark flying.

Impenetrable, the outside
door is locked by feathered code.

They are guarding in sharp murders,
preemptive bombardments of black.

They arrived last year, when we
bridged water, so did their wings.

It beckoned them, a beacon
for harassment, for shipping harm.

They caused a catastrophic spill,
oil, from a grounded tanker.

Fleets crash on this route, compasses
and maps fogged with misguidance.

Gasses, guns, nothing curtailed
their calls of nested harmony.

Hopeless, we concede to their sound
shadow, their bloody cloak, cawing.

FALL FISHING

There is a drought, and the salmon
people, unable to seine water,
wake it, fish out river, withdrawn.

Evergreens are forked in dust,
with boulders cracking like bone spurs,
spurring the thirst of it, the well.

Fish decay in there, while men dig
for meat, making a maelstrom
of sand and sun, summer fervor.

They build a ladder in hot light,
reaching a summit to summon
clouds, gray yellow, and thunder it.

Gutting, they make a sea of sky,
funnel clouds, and squall storming,
to summon a wet season: fall.

It pours like mother's milk, forming
roe flourish, the living spawn
of seasonal change, their feeding.

SWEET BITE

Maple mosquito bite,
it oozes insect goo
into a trench of arms,
trove of tree infection.

Bubble brown, the insect
molds a sour sugar,
impossible tapping
of a sickening sweet.

A boy discovers it,
lured by the lumpy awe
of its shimmering cake,
its crest of buggy sheen.

He bites the organic
entrails of gruesome
shine, sticky, like taffy
of viral flight, filling.

His stomach of a sting
digests crunchy candy,
full of its brackish bite,
insecticide, inside.

DISEMBARK

Inorganic orca, netted
in noose of fishing lines
and pots of crab torture,
it moans in mucous spouts
of sickening sea, caught
in selfie culture, girls
with peace fingers, awash
in social media soup
of ocean emojis,
pictures of cruising ports,
and gawks mocking whale gape,
desperate, calling sea
to water its oil, steal
skin away, to wake it
in tidal draw, offshore,
while it spoils in sinking
under the farewell pier
of click-it-y-clack pics
with a cutout cousin
of the killer below,
tourists waving goodbye.

SCOURGE

Redbelly cooters, tortured turtles
in our field of cabbages, carrots, beets,
becoming a horde of devilish domes
in scattered mist, munching like shredders,
inhaling life out of darkness, to light.

So we bought a beast, a fierce Rottweiler
to ravage them, rout out the pests, upheave
bodies in monstrous bedlam, bludgeoning
into a great morgue of reptile mountain,
hooded, with ornamental shells of gore.

Over vegetables, it has had enough
and transforms to werewolf with hunting cap
made from carapace carnage, eyeing us
and coming, because humans are tender,
perfect for evening entrails, mortal meat.

THE SOUND OF TWILIGHT

Wolves howl a chorus of ogres
under rising of summer moon,
cratered, with craggy repel
of cacophonous barks, biting
distance between us, in wolf trap.

So we carry arrows and spears
to skewer their scare to silence;
then gramophone skips, and a girl
flees into mist, muting music
of demons, her derivatives.

To an enchantress in twilight
with tulip tiara, icicle wand,
lily slippers, beautified beast,
she casts an enrapture, shooting
our silver bullet to sonic.

NEIGHBORLY

Ravine wardrobe of waste
where septic water spreads
into bramble beavers,
building a dam of rank,
rotten, like wet sulfur,
where vermin spout its spring
into odorous havoc,
hurling a sewer stench
up our neighbor's nostrils
to bore his puny brain
of reckless weed killer,
which father refused
to scatter here, hiding
his secretive soldiers
of poo, pulverizing
their sewage sand, players
beneath the cranky calls
of wrinkled curmudgeon;
so dad decides to dig
with those odorous pests,
releasing wicked ew
for that old man's ugly,
his bastardly bother
of disgusting insults,
insulated in cloak
when father found stinkers
reveling, our revenge.

RENASCENCE

SIDEWALK SALT

Ionized compound
with an equal ratio
of sodium and chloride,
it wastes an earthworm
with osmotic shrinkage,
sidewalk suck, knowing
nothing of skin, organs,
carbon dioxide; it drains
worm away. Watch it
concreted, shriveling
without heels to spike
relentless sun, caught
between sky and soil,
without compost mixing
an elemental afterlife,
compound of recycled
fruit, with delicious apple
tree above this mound
of white, speckled gray,
salted, clinging to shoes.

PEOPLE IN THE SUN
-after Edward Hopper

Beneath a blue, so vast
skyscrapers could not
block viewing, there are
five tourists waiting,
wanting a vivid wind
to blow prairie gold
into mountainous brown,
browner than Chicago
smog, rising from golden
wheat that rolls naturally
within air streaming
scents of buffalo hides
and fuming native
fires, wolves that wander
in search of roaming fowl,
rabbits, and muskrat meat
in swift tumbleweeds
of gathering wild
American West, bound
in a ball of the best
view outside of city
life and drycleaner
steam, stuff of cotton
burns and molten neckties,
like these people in sun,
sitting here, holding on
to worn arms, unrested
by tourists, seated,
taunted, breathless, baited
and ready for something

like Lake Michigan flood
across Golden Coast
and Magnificent Mile,
in this place of pulsing
hearts, desperate, craving
that moment of brush
across serene, scape
where deer and antelope
play and skies are
not cloudy all day.

WILDERNESS RENTAL

The cabin has a sunset view,
cabana chairs, and tree hammocks
for lounging with the animals.

Tiki torches carefully placed
beside the hot tub, grill, and bar
mark luau nights in wilderness.

With furnished guest rooms, bathrooms,
and kitchen, it is a rugged
experience with bald eagles.

Guests will see reindeer, bears, falcons,
huskies, orcas, salmon, and whales
from a private beach and fire pit.

Ice is available, but guests
mostly prefer fresh glacier
water for frozen daiquiris.

Electricity and water
are included, along with free
fish gummies for the little ones.

Free nights, if booked in advance,
along with wild welcome gifts,
to live in nature for sale.

OLD SOUNDS

Pink into white, with beige trimming,
boys are painting our building today
with a modern look so moving
it can romance millennials
to its contemporary twist, cubic
like a motherboard's build, crisp
under legacy starlings, nested
above since the nineties, our roof
a reception of bird nuisance,
noisy chorus of sharpened flats
beloved for their belligerence,
bombarding constant cacophony
for home defense, their duty
done today as they terrorize
the young with marauding muse
of nonsensical sound, nested,
as boys refuse to roost, running
away from calls of old ages,
escaping to a pubescent place
where sound is giddy and wee.

LUAU FEET

Polynesian poster
of a bunion-less man,
toenails clipped, manicured,
with a polish of pearls
over sand, massaging
his toes, fanned, across
a plumeria beach, white,

and illuminated
by macadamia mounds,
with milk of coconut
sheen, and crowns of ginger,
granting a glimpse of feet,
unfettered, unfurled,
in paradise, without

designer shoes and silk
stockings, the strangling kind,
that torture our toes, stick
into nails, overgrown,
cutting in callused prints
of skins, waiting in tow,
for a podiatrist

who shows us the smiling
face of a flame thrower
native who never wears
heels or unfitted shoes,
but rather worships fire
when walking across coals
from his volcanic flow

because he has perfect
feet, swift, ready to dance,
as you limp away, lost,
in a tropical trance
of luxurious luau,
imprinted for ingrowns,
to party away pain.

GRAFFITI

Sunday, he saw his first
graffiti after church
on a cloverleaf bridge
to home, his familiar
highway, but different,
contrasting shined shoes,
his fitted service suit,
where a curvaceous tag
of obese ovals, round
rectangles, sunken squares,
as if an elephant
was driven over, hit,
then planted into road,
inelegant, unfit,
yet curious; he traces
ordered disorder,
its animal lines, wild
sprays of gray and blue hues
that run over concrete
and underpass arches,
calculated chaos
for byways of blurred
birches, pines, magnolias,
smeared by cars speeding
in their late laziness;
and he sees this awkward
tumor, forcing his eyes
to believe disbelief,
that god would allow
this divine creation
to live in a causeway,
cutting, embellished.

NIGHT MASK

In alarming night, he sees moths
flutter like eyelashes, awake,
disrupting sleep, his nuisance.

They are his nocturnal, nightly
disease, constant, incurable,
not even by insect killer.

In this sudden palace of white
streptococci, milky splatter
of mask, he suffocates.

Blinded, breathless, unbeatable,
he fleshes his face, scraping skin
into desperate peels, off.

But away, his ended nightmare
of eternal insecticide,
he scars in the black, blooded air.

Dark brightens in morning, its light
clearing the room of sickly wings,
in his sunny disposition.

PLAYGROUND SCIENCE

A colony under convex, it caves
in relentless sun, intolerable

cruelty, magnified, kinetic.
For a boy in scientific body,

an optical engineer, he studies
electromagnetic radiation

in his execution experiment.
Ants become illicit in yellow heat,

cremating their black away, spotlighted.
Pensive, he pauses, wondering why light

can be so hostile, yet wonderful
in burning, ionic enlightenment.

POWER HITTER

Electric egret, it transforms
a transformer to bird fryer,
with energy station nearby
to enlighten its fall, so bright
for the batting boy to slam it
with nuclear power, homer nuke
to broken wings, legs, yellow bill,
belligerent atomic bust
to see if birdie bones fissure
in lanes on electric avenue
of his fallen fowl, radiating
flown spoils of powerful pulses
across his street of shocks, plumed
by rainbow rain, chemical clouds,
gauze of carbonic birding dress
to play a plutonium ballgame,
betting he'll beat the toxic smoke
with birds of radiation, hitting
against the neighborhood demon
of illness, illicit villain
against nevermore wings, his bats
of darkness, smashing power down
with athletic prowess, winged,
whacking cloud cancer, with feathers.

LADYBUGS

She reaches into their red, becoming
a body of them, spotted and shining
in leaves at school, her dawn of dissection,
eating summer's afterlife in fall, fresh,
with antenna, elytra, eyes, thorax:
biology lesson before the bell, learning
how insects morph in color's masquerade,
caught, in a story for class, shown, and told.

MONARCH

A girl flicks off orange
ones, saying their sickly
wings resemble rotten
fruit from groves of icky
peels and putrid seeds.

They are smelly, spotted
black and white, and flying
like her turbulent stroll
in this lavish kingdom
of blooms, pollinated.

And sneezy, the breezes
becoming airborne plagues
of insects, insulting
her prowess, her power,
inhaling gold, she gasps.

Monarchs, zebras, cloudless
sulfurs, supposedly
indigenous, they are
a nuisance, constantly
disheveling ringlets.

Of styled hair, perfect
for a princess party
after this garden tour
of her royal greenhouse,
she prefers pink lilies.

Yellows and blues bother
her, but like a precious
pillow of silk, sultry,
the pink caresses her,
hands vanquishing butters.

BURIED IN BERRIES

The boysenberry boy
is jamming again, jaw
deep into purple patch,
fingers fumbling on.

And over his buckets
he bites into wild
weeds, the ones we sent him
to whack, his sweet welcome.

Not our plague, to him,
but rather a purple
people eater to juice, in jest.
he bats the red out of them.

All color into cakes
of seeds and sediment,
with a river of blood,
to drink natural dirge.

To lap it up, in love
with our garden creeper,
he eats sugar for free,
for his fruition.

Finished, there are none
left, only their leaves;
so we apologize,
thanking him, for the fight.

DOG BIRD

Wild stork, it sees salmon in us,
avoiding peas, our frozen feed,
in morning, instead watching lips
lick Coho, sockeye, coveted
fish, fresh, smoking in scrumptious air.

Swallowing, we suck up the meat
into organs, stomach to intestine,
colonizing colons, lacquered
by brine and seasoned oil, blood
becoming a brothel of lure.

Into us, peck for every bite,
it will become a wolf, feathers
to fur, molting away its frock
of white, transforming into brown,
making its beast in us, no bill,
to eat digested eyes, bladders.

This is no bird, but a diving
monster with claws, coo into bark,
eyes bound to full bodies, sizing
us up for feeding; but instead
it flies away, for fresher fish.

INGRAINED

Pillow wheat, it wakens
underneath overalls
and field boots, beaten

by the harvesting dredge
of a man in sweat, sun
beating down his setting.

It is summer, and he
holds a scythe, slicing heads
with curvaceous blade

to make a maelstrom
of land mattress, to quake
folds of fibrous gold.

He molds a pot of arms,
reaching into riches,
his horde of heavy work.

He refuses to rinse
fingers, instead fitting
his wealth, germinated.

HEROIC HOOKER

He insisted on ice
for catching unfrozen
fish, fresh, underwater
in winter, for frosted
fins, swim bladders, and gills,
gaping at walleye man,
champion of fishermen
with gold medals galore,
dangling from trophy glitz
in his cabin of soul,
where shine never faded,
until he slid within
swallow of mighty catch,
giant with gargantuan gape
and incisor army
for munching mealworm man
and his pathetic pole
with golden weaves of line,
shimmering silver hooks,
caught, in wee intestines,
where hero washed out.

BIRDING OIL

Irresistible sheen, it is
inedible for an eagle
which slips on it, sliding away
for a taste of a sea eel,
cloaked in black burden, a caulk.

Hunger, it hinders a curved beak,
biting into black, dark torture
of earth, matted spout; it bit
the head, its flock of white feathers
and razor eyes, eyeing the cake.

Where its mother discovers it
mired, pitted, within a well
of sky souls, beach of drowning birds,
she rips it up, tears its tethers
to hear the calling, free its caw.

From oil, sanded into sludge,
the boy ascends in wind, breaking
away into the blue solace
of home, high above overspill,
its mother encaged in claws.

ANT CARPENTER

He is hacking away wood ants
for the family in them, the views
of a wilderness moon, children

with marshmallows, and a woman
who watches him working, his back
to insect bites, eyes engaged.

He will marry her, make their nest
a tribute to tree colonies,
milled to lumber cathedrals,

places to worship his offspring
of roots, perpetual biters
in a mandible logging mill.

And they become one, a body
of antennae, thoraces, eyes,
married ants, from leveled larvae.

CAST AWAY

We built a boat today, wooden
and without a power motor.

Rudders, transoms, and hulls,
father drew dimensions for us.

And we made it with a wheel
of cedar and steel handholds.

Stern to bow, hull to mast, it rises
like wakes in naval attire.

It is better than us, our ground
of pavement and cracking driveway.

Slingshots, slides, inflatable pools
fill cave in here, like sealant.

Lounges, mattresses, mothballed
pillows, all stuff our land cancer.

Radials, transmissions, oils,
sparks, they plug in ages, bankrupt.

So we seal our past, sails
hoisted, naming it *The Away.*

LOAM

Our sand, silt, and clay composite
is ready for plowing in rows

of organic wheat, where we stretch
our toes in soil, for its soothing

warmth in a field of memories,
where we planted before winter

in our permanent sow of wealth,
cultivated, ready to grow

into eternal feed, for life,
where mechanical grain grinders

mill away all natural meals
for market, for the bottom line;

but we refuse to mechanize
into the overprocessed

today, instead walking within
our solid roots, our family core

of crowns, tillers, leaves, our living,
devoured, eaten, earthen.

ACKNOWLEDGMENTS

"XO Taste" *Plainsongs*

"How Grownups Fire" *The Fourth River*

"Osteology" *Barely South Review*

"Painful Reminder" *Pif Magazine*

"Sidewalk Salt" *Bombay Gin*

"Wilderness Rental" *The Wayfarer*

"Playground Science" *City of Orlando*

"Ladybugs" *City of Orlando*

"Ingrained" *Freshwater*

"Cast Away" *Valparaiso Poetry Review*

"Loam" *The Wayfarer*

"Hercules," "Wicked Pool," "Serenity Lake," published by Orange County, Florida in visual arts exhibition: *Orange County Poets: From Within and Wonder*

I would like to thank my family and friends in Seattle, Washington DC, Baltimore, and Middlebury for helping make this poetry collection possible. Johns Hopkins and the Bread Loaf Writers' Conference will forever inspire my poetic craft and studies. Thank you to the *New York Journal of Books* for publishing my poetry reviews to encourage others to write, study, and analyze poetry. Ted Kooser's feedback and ideas have inspired me to continue publishing poetry critiques and supporting my fellow poets.

ABOUT THE AUTHOR

Andrew Jarvis is the author of *The Strait, Landslide,* and *Blood Moon.* His poems have appeared in *Cottonwood, Measure, The Fourth River, Valparaiso Poetry Review,* and many others. He holds high honors from the Nautilus, INDIE Book of the Year, and NextGen Indie Book Awards. Andrew holds an M.A. in Writing from Johns Hopkins University and has been writing only poetry for more than 20 years. He lives in Orlando, FL, where alligators invade his backyard.

WAYFARER

BASED IN THE BERKSHIRE MOUNTAINS, MASS.

The Wayfarer Magazine. Since 2012, *The Wayfarer* has been offering literature, interviews, and art with the intention to inspires our readers, enrich their lives, and highlight the power for agency and change-making that each individual holds. By our definition, a wayfarer is one whose inner-compass is ever-oriented to truth, wisdom, healing, and beauty in their own wandering. The Wayfarer's mission as a publication is to foster a community of contemplative voices and provide readers with resources and perspectives that support them in their own journey.

Wayfarer Books is our newest imprint! After nearly 10 years in print, *The Wayfarer Magazine* is branching out from our magazine to become a full-fledged publishing house offering full-length works of eco-literature!

Wayfarer Farm & Retreat is our latest endeavor, springing up the Berkshire Mountains of Massachusetts. Set to open to the public in 2024, the 15 acre retreat will offer workshops, farm-to-table dinners, off-grid retreat cabins, and artist residencies.

WWW.WAYFARERBOOKS.ORG

CPSIA information can be obtained
at www.ICGtesting.com
Printed in the USA
BVHW070208100322
630962BV00003B/201